HARMONIZING 'BACH' CHORALES

MALCOLM BOYD

Harmonizing 'Bach' Chorales

BARRIE & JENKINS

London Melbourne Sydney Auckland Johannesburg

Barrie and Jenkins Ltd
An imprint of the Hutchinson Publishing Group
3 Fitzroy Square, London W1P 6JD

Hutchinson Group (Australia) Pty Ltd
30–32 Cremorne Street, Richmond South, Victoria 3121
PO Box 151, Broadway, New South Wales 2007

Hutchinson Group (NZ) Ltd
32–34 View Road, PO Box 40–086, Glenfield, Auckland 10

Hutchinson Group (SA) (Pty) Ltd
PO Box 337, Bergvlei 2012, South Africa

© Malcolm Boyd 1967

First published in 1967 by Barrie and Rockliff
Reprinted in 1977 and 1980 by Barrie & Jenkins Ltd

Printed in Great Britain by The Anchor Press Ltd
Tiptree, Essex

ISBN 0 214 65956 9

CONTENTS

INTRODUCTION

The imitation of Bach's chorale harmonizations has for long, and rightly, been considered an instructive part of a musician's general training. Students themselves nearly always find it stimulating to write 'real' music and to be able to match their efforts not against arbitrary textbook examples, but against music by one of the great composers. This applies even to those for whom the exercise remains purely one of imitation, but the more gifted student will find that the restrictions which a given style imposes will stimulate his invention, perhaps even to the extent of entirely original composition, not necessarily in the same style.

The success of the study will depend to a great extent on how well the given style has been assimilated by the student, and indeed it is largely towards this assimilation that the exercise is directed. Too often the imitations fall short of their models not through any lack of innate musicianship on the student's part, but because Bach's methods have been inadequately studied and insufficiently understood. Harmony textbooks are not always helpful here either, and sometimes misleading. It is not enough to know that such-and-such a procedure is sanctioned by Bach; the student (if he is to produce harmony and texture at all resembling Bach's) must have some idea also of how often it occurs, in what contexts, and, if possible, why. In other words, he must be able to distinguish the typical from the exceptional so that he may know what to imitate and what to avoid in his own attempts to reproduce Bach's chorale style.

The present booklet, in attempting to help the student in this way, presupposes some experience in 'traditional' harmony on his part. It assumes also that he knows how and when to modulate and that he is aware of the nature and function of passing notes, suspensions, and appoggiaturas. The writer's intention is to guide the student in his own investigation of the Bach chorales, and to assist him to reproduce Bachian harmony and texture by drawing attention to those features which distinguish Bach's style. It is *not* his intention to present ready-made formulae for writing 'Bach' chorales, and it is most important that the present booklet should be used side by side with a volume of Bach chorales—never as a replacement for it.

In order to encourage and facilitate this kind of study the reader is frequently referred to examples in the '371' chorales by Bach. Numerical references in the text are to Albert Riemenschneider's edition, published by Schirmer/Chappell.[1] Quantitative analyses are based on the chorales in this volume, omitting those which present duplicate harmonizations, of which there are about twenty-four. Another eleven harmonizations have not been considered here, either because they go beyond the normal chorale style in their texture and figuration (see chorales nos. 270 and 283), or because they are unusually long and elaborate (chorales nos. 132 and 205). Also omitted from the analysis is no. 150, both because it is a unique five-part setting and because it is not by Bach. Figures and tables quoted in the booklet are therefore based upon analysis of the remaining 335 chorales, excluding all repeats.

[1] This is the text most commonly used today, in Great Britain at least. Readers with other editions are referred to Appendix on page 40.

MELODIC CHARACTERISTICS OF THE CHORALE

Before beginning to harmonize a chorale (or any other melody for that matter), the student should pause to consider its salient musical characteristics. The term 'chorale' itself need cause no bewilderment; it is more or less synonymous with our 'hymn tune', and both chorales and hymn tunes exist in great variety. There are certain features, however, which serve to distinguish the chorale from other types of hymn tune, and which make the retention of the German term desirable and on the whole more meaningful than our use of the word *Lieder* for German songs. Since melodic features will partly determine the kind of harmony to be used, it will not be out of place to preface our investigation of Bach's chorale harmony with some remarks upon the nature of the chorales themselves.

This is not the place for a history of Lutheran hymnody, and it need not concern us now that some of the attributes we are about to describe were not necessarily characteristic of the chorale before Bach's time. It is worth pointing out, however, that only a few of the melodies which Bach harmonized and used so extensively in his music were actually written by him. Many of the Lutheran hymn tunes can be traced back to the more popular plainsong melodies of pre-Reformation times, and their modality is often still apparent. Others again were adapted from secular origins, or 'stolen from the Devil' as Luther himself would have it. Of these the best known is undoubtedly the so-called 'Passion' chorale, familiar to most English-speaking congregations as 'O sacred head sore wounded'. This famous tune first appeared in a volume of love songs by Hassler, printed in 1601. Still other melodies were specially written in the two centuries following the Reformation, but by Bach's time interest in chorale composition had largely died out. Interest in the reharmonization of the old melodies, however, was never keener.

During the two hundred years which preceded Bach's appointment as cantor at St Thomas's Church, Leipzig, the chorale had quite naturally undergone many changes. The most important of these was that it had lost most of the metrical freedom associated with its earliest period in favour of a steady movement in crotchets and minims, with occasional quavers as passing notes. The typical chorale melody as Bach found it proceeded in a regular $\frac{4}{4}$ metre, usually with one syllable to each note; $\frac{3}{4}$ metre is not uncommon, however, and sometimes both $\frac{4}{4}$ and $\frac{3}{4}$ metres are found in the same chorale (see chorale no. 11). The impression of strength and solidity which this steady rhythmic 'tread' conveys is intensified by a melodic line which combines a preponderance of stepwise movement with an insistence on primary intervals (fourths and fifths). The chorales which embody these melodic and rhythmic features accord well with recurrent Lutheran images of God or Christ as a rock, a fortress, a shield—*ein feste Burg*, in fact. Their very style is like a profession of faith.

The melodic characteristics of the chorale should exert their influence on the kind of harmony and texture one chooses to support it. In the first place, one has to ensure that each of the added parts—alto, tenor, and bass —has sufficient notes for the number of syllables sung by the soprano. Ideally the student should be given the words as well, for these too ought to influence his harmonizations as they certainly influenced Bach's. For practical reasons it is perhaps wise not to insist upon this, but the student should always bear in mind that the parts he is writing are intended to be sung, and for the most part with a change of syllable every crotchet.

Secondly, one must recognize that the crotchet tread of the melody will determine the rate of chord change in the harmony. In fact there will usually be a change of chord (or position of the chord) with every crotchet beat; quavers will, in general, be treated as passing notes, and minims will be harmonized with more than one chord. It may be taken as a general principle that repetition of a chord from a weak to a strong beat will halt the pulse of the music, and this rule is not invalidated by certain exceptions which will be described in a later paragraph.

Finally, the student must endeavour in his treatment of the chorale to match melodic strength with harmonic firmness. The method of achieving this will be the subject of a later section, but it is worth pointing out here that the student needs no particularly advanced knowledge of harmony to begin a study of Bach's chorale style. A good grasp of the formation and function of simple triads and of the dominant seventh is all that should be required in the way of harmonic resource; it is a very simple matter to assimilate the supertonic seventh needed at cadences, and idiomatic use of the diminished seventh soon comes with observation and practice. The cadences provide the pillars for the harmonic structure, and it is towards these that our attention should first be directed.

CADENCES

A glance at any Bach chorale will show a number of pause marks placed above certain notes in the melody. These sometimes puzzle the student at first, particularly when he finds that they are by no means always observed in performance. They are, of course, intended merely as a guide to the singers, and indicate the ends of lines in the text in much the same way as do the double bar lines in most English hymnals. A pause at such places will, in fact, be both appropriate and desirable in most cases, and when it comes to harmonizing a chorale we can normally regard the pause marks as indicating cadence points.

It is most instructive to study carefully the cadence points in Bach's harmonizations, and to observe how carefully the modulations are planned and the cadences chosen to produce the utmost variety without impairing the basic strength of the harmony. As we might expect, perfect cadences predominate because they are required to establish modulation. And root position chords are used far more frequently than inversions because they serve to strengthen the harmony at those places where strength is most needed. The extent of this predominance is clearly shown in the following table, which summarizes the findings of an analysis of all the cadences in the '371' chorales:

Cadence	Root position	Inverted	Total	Approximate Percentage
Perfect (V–I)	1,241	211	1,452	73
Imperfect (?–V)	225	190	415	21
Plagal (IV–I)	30	14	44	2
Interrupted (V–VI)	33	nil	33	1·5
Others (including the final cadences of modal chorales)			50	2·5

The insistence on perfect cadences in root position contributes in no small measure to the overall strength of the harmony, and plagal cadences, with their altogether 'softer' effect, are comparatively little used. Imperfect cadences are, of course, indispensable and, since they come to rest on the dominant, in no way detract from the vigour of the harmony. The small proportion (1·5 per cent) of interrupted closes is rather surprising perhaps, and deserves careful notice. In spite of their usefulness for avoiding undesirable full closes in many contexts, they are on the whole foreign to Bach's chorale style. Most of them, though not all, are to be found in one or another of the following contexts:

   (a) As a penultimate cadence when the melody would otherwise invite a full close *in the home key.* See nos. 15, 60, 122, 176, 183, 184, 219, 238, and 241.

   (b) In a succession of two or three very short lines, where the unvarying use of perfect cadences would tend to break up too much the flow of the music. See chorales nos. 179, 278, 321, and 360.

   (c) In very long chorales, where a greater variety of cadential progressions is naturally more desirable. See chorales nos. 214, 215, 241, and 296.

Unless he is quite certain that it would come into one of these three categories, the student should think again before using an interrupted cadence in a 'Bach' chorale.

Still more to be avoided are any cadences demanding the use of the dominant 13th, or what some textbooks refer to as the first inversion of the mediant chord (IIIb). The chord evidently held no attraction for Bach in this context, and cadential progressions like that in example 1 are very rare

Example 1

[No. 181]

II'b   V¹³
[III b]

indeed. Bach's usual practice in such cases is to modulate to the relative minor (in example 1 this would be to E minor); occasionally, however, he will choose to treat the first note of the cadence as a leading note and make an unexpected move to the subdominant, with the leading note proceeding to the fifth of the next chord (see example 2). The progression is not a common one, and occurs in all less than a score of times in the '371'; it is

Example 2

[No. 1]

nevertheless characteristic, and the student might like to experiment with it from time to time.

Our investigations into Bach's cadences show that, except in imperfect cadences, inversions are greatly outnumbered by root position chords. Moreover, when an inverted cadence *is* used it is almost invariably the first of the two chords which is inverted. Inversion of the pause chord itself is *most unusual*; there are only nineteen instances of it in the nineteen hundred cadences analysed. No doubt the reason is, once again, to achieve the maximum harmonic strength. A few of those which are inverted are dominant sevenths, and there is even one diminished seventh (see chorale no. 327), but on the whole the student would be well advised to use only root position for the pause chords.

Another feature of the pause chord is worth stressing here. Its function as a pillar in the harmonic framework of the chorale is further strengthened by making the chord complete—that is to say, including the fifth as well as the root and the third. This is not an invariable rule, but it does apply to more than ninety-five per cent of Bach's cadences, and is therefore one which the student who aims at a typical harmonization might well regard as invariable. Although, as we have already hinted, observation of the pause in performance will depend largely upon the sense of the text, Bach evidently wanted the harmony at such places to sound as sonorous as possible, and chorale no. 100, in which all six pause chords are incomplete (i.e. lacking the fifth of the harmony) is in this respect most unusual indeed.

Some good reason for the omission of the fifth is usually quite evident to the investigator in those cases where Bach has left it out; often it has been done to avoid consecutive fifths.

Filling out the pause chord in this way frequently makes it impossible for the leading note at the cadence to proceed to the tonic, and the student must here unlearn one of the most common of textbook precepts. In such cases, the leading note will usually fall a third (as in examples 1, 3(b), 3(c), 3(d), 7(a), 7(b), and 8(b)), but it is not uncommon for it to rise to the third of the chord which follows, even when a minor key results in the interval of a diminished fourth (see examples 3(a) and 5). Other resolutions of the leading note are also found, but they are not common and need not be shown here. It is important to note that which ever way the leading note proceeds at a cadence, it is quite wrong to insert passing notes between it and the note which follows. For instance, in example 3(c) the student might be tempted to write a passing note between the G sharp and the E in the alto part; this is *never* found in Bach's work.

Suspensions, a feature of Bach's chorale style in general, should seldom be used at the end of a line. As a rule, Bach makes all the parts halt together at the pause chord, and the student who writes to follow Bach's example in this will introduce a suspension at such places only once in about twenty-five cadences, and reserve most of them for the more elaborate treatment of longer chorales. It is perhaps necessary to add that passing notes will be used between the pause chord and the one which follows it only by those who have forgotten that there are words to be sung.

The crotchet rate of chord change should not be relaxed at the cadences until the pause itself is reached. The inexperienced student will often arrive at the dominant chord too soon, especially where there is a minim in the melody immediately before the pause. In such cases the minim should be harmonized with two chords (as in examples 3(a), 3(c), and 3(d)) or with a suspension resolving into the dominant chord (as in example 6(d)).

The chord of the supertonic seventh, especially in its first inversion (II⁷ b), is so commonly found as the approach to a perfect cadence in both major and minor keys that the student would be well advised to memorize the progression and to reproduce it on most of the occasions which permit its use. It is most frequently found in the simple form which we see at example 7(a), and always with the seventh itself prepared in the previous chord. Example 1 shows a slightly embroidered version, and some other variants may be observed in example 3. Examples 3(c) and 3(d) show the supertonic seventh in its chromatic form—that is with the third of the chord sharpened (and also the fifth in a minor key). This chromatic form is by no means uncommon in the Bach chorales, although it occurs less frequently than the plain diatonic form. Perhaps its most useful function

Example 3

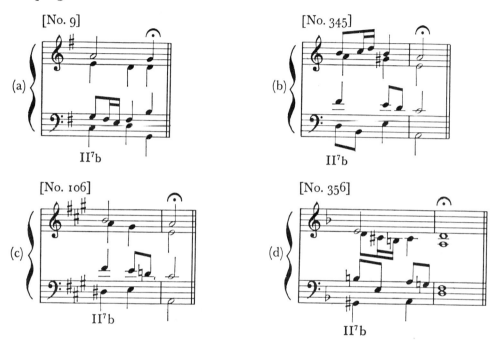

is to avoid exact repetition of a cadence already used earlier in a chorale.

On the subject of cadences there remains to be mentioned only the fact that the final chords of all chorales, including modal and minor ones, are almost invariably major.

HARMONIC RESOURCE

Cadences have been discussed at some length because their proper treatment is absolutely essential for a successful imitation of Bach's style. If the student takes care in preparing the modulations, the cadences, and their approaches, he will find that the rest of the harmony often falls into place with little trouble.

It has already been mentioned that the steady metre and the strong melodic contours of the chorales themselves should be matched in the harmony chosen to support them. This means, in technical terms, placing great reliance on major and minor triads and generally avoiding those chords which produce a 'weaker' effect—particularly diminished triads, and the dominant 7th in root position. Bach's harmony, it is true, goes far beyond these limited resources, but it is wrong to suppose that he used sevenths and chromatic chords in any profusion. Many of us begin with a false idea of Bach's chorale harmony precisely because those of his harmonizations which most readily commend themselves for the emotional response they arouse in us are the least typical. The student will go astray if he attempts to base his chorale style on some of those in the *St Matthew Passion* or on particularly chromatic ones elsewhere (chorale no. 216 for example), no matter how much he may prefer them to more run-of-the-mill harmonizations. Analysis of chorales selected at random from the '371' will soon demonstrate how basically simple Bach's harmony is for the most part. Indeed it is to be recommended that the student should make harmonic analyses of a few chorales before attempting harmonizations of his own. He will probably be astonished to find how far Bach restricts himself to the common major and minor triads. The use of more advanced chords will often be possible, but rarely desirable. The student should aim, therefore, at a strong and fairly simple harmonization, remembering that uncomplicated harmony will give the best chance of achieving the kind of texture that is typical of Bach's style.

Chorales which open with an anacrusis often cause some difficulty when they do not permit the use of V–I harmony over the bar-line. The student who has been correctly taught to change the chord from a weak to a strong beat will go to enormous lengths to avoid opening with two statements of the tonic chord in root position. And yet this is just what Bach does in most cases. In fact, he prefers to open like this even when the melody would permit the use of chords V–I. To repeat a chord over the bar-line is inevitably to rob the first beat of the bar of some of its strength, and it is usually advisable to compensate for this loss of accent, where possible, by writing higher notes in the second chord than in the first. The effect of this in performance will be to make the chord on the strong beat sound louder and more sonorous, and for this reason example 4(a) is to be preferred to example 4(b), although both are by Bach.

Example 4

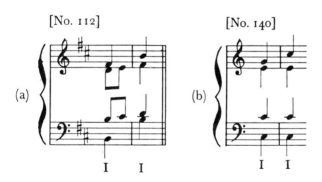

The repetition of a chord from a weak to a strong beat can be applied, in principle, to the beginning of any line of the melody, not necessarily the first. Apart from such places, however, the harmony should continually move forwards towards the next cadence. It is essential, therefore, that the cadences should have been carefully worked out in advance, so that the student (and the listener, even if he is an imaginary being) is quite certain where the harmony is leading.

UNESSENTIAL NOTES

While Bach's harmony is basically quite simple in the chorales, his use of unessential material is always resourceful, and sometimes quite complex. It is true that some chorale harmonizations (for example nos. 102 and 327) contain few unessential notes or none at all, but such chorales (most of them, for some reason, in $\frac{3}{4}$ metre) are not at all typical. The majority make use of all the possibilities which passing notes and suspensions offer to give variety and richness to the part-writing, and it is by the texture, as well as by the harmony itself, that we recognize the distinctive chorale style.

The invigorating effect of accented passing notes should not be overlooked; too often they are forgotten by students who would never miss the opportunity to use a suspension or an unaccented passing note. The genuine appoggiatura (an accented dissonance approached by leap), on the other hand, is entirely foreign to Bach's chorale style. That he was fully aware of the expressive nature of the appoggiatura is amply demonstrated in other works where the context demands a yearning or sighing feeling, but such expression is, as I have been at pains to point out, quite at variance with the character of the Lutheran chorale. The G sharp in the tenor line of example 5 could be regarded as an appoggiatura resolving into a cadential $\frac{6}{4}$ chord, and a few progressions like this one do occur in the '371'. Other examples

Example 5

of appoggiaturas in either melody or added parts are so rare that the student will be wise to leave aside appoggiaturas altogether when imitating the Bach style.

On the whole, Bach follows fairly closely the rule and practice of his day that weak quavers, other than harmony notes, should move by step. Notes of anticipation are fairly common at cadences, but rare elsewhere. The *échappée* is found at cadences, too (see example 6(a)), and the *cambiata* figure is sometimes seen (see example 6(b)), but neither is very common. Other apparent exceptions to the general rule governing quaver movement can often be explained by reference to other parts in the harmony. The opening of chorale no.149, for instance, shows a progression which is by no means unique in Bach's chorale harmonizations (see example 6(c)). It seems at first glance that the soprano C in this example is contravening the

Example 6

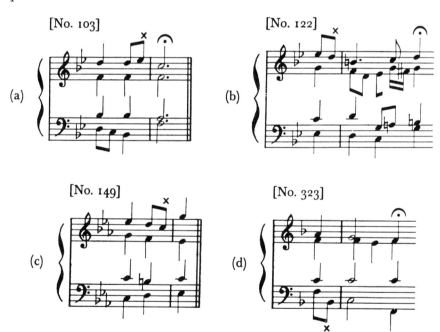

general rule that dissonant quavers should not be quitted by leap, and certainly most textbooks would advise the student to treat the soprano D as an accented passing note. The argument is, of course, that this is just what Bach *has* done. The alto and bass notes in the second chord can be regarded as passing notes and the tenor B as an auxiliary note. This means that the soprano C is, in fact, the only harmony note and its progression by leap therefore quite orthodox.

This might seem a rather laboured defence of a passage which is, after all, quite easy for the ear to accept, and the truth is that Bach himself is unlikely to have thought about it in this way. But it is precisely the absence of any similar explanation which makes the passage shown in example 6(d) far less acceptable to the ear, to the singer, and to the student who aims to write in Bach's style.

CONSECUTIVES

The most interesting and instructive aspect of Bach's treatment of consecutive fifths and octaves in the chorales is not so much the way he uses them as the means he uses to avoid them. He has sometimes been credited with a far less stringent attitude towards consecutives than is the case. The only instance where he regularly permitted himself consecutive fifths was when a note of anticipation at a cadence coincided with the dominant seventh in a lower part (see example 7(a)). Chorale no. 8 shows no less than four such

Example 7

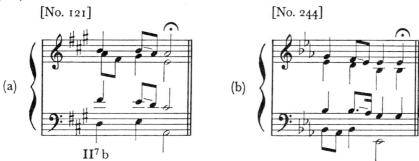

progressions, although in fact the procedure is far less common than it might have been, and its effect is frequently mollified by delaying the dominant seventh until after the note of anticipation (as in example 7(b)).

There is no truth in the suggestion which some authorities make that Bach was indulgent towards consecutives appearing at the end of one line and the beginning of the next. It is true that a few instances of this are to be found in the '371', and one might mention here chorales nos. 70, 134, 164, 243, 269, 334, and 368. What is sometimes forgotten, or not understood, is that many of the '371' chorales are taken from cantatas (including some which are now lost) and that in the originals each line of the chorale was separated from the next by an instrumental passage. When these instrumental passages are removed, as they were for the purpose of inclusion in the '371', consecutives often appear in the vocal parts where, in the original, they do not exist. There can be little doubt that Bach himself would have removed the consecutives if he had intended to perform the chorales as we find them in the '371'.

The strength of the evidence, indeed, suggests that he went to considerable pains to avoid consecutives in such places. Sometimes he did this by omitting the fifth from the pause chord, sometimes by making the parts cross (see example 9(a)), and sometimes by a complete re-arrangement of the voice parts (see chorale no. 297).

Apart from those which occur with anticipatory notes in the soprano and the easily explained occurences between the lines of a chorale, there remain some examples of consecutive fifths which are not easy to account for. But isolated instances (for they are indeed rare) should not tempt us to imitate a practice of which there is ample evidence to show Bach's disapproval. When we come across consecutives like those in example 8 our first suspicions should be that either the text is at these points corrupt, or that Bach has not spotted the consecutives and would have corrected them if he had.

Example 8

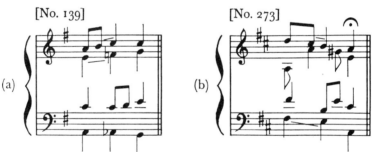

There are, in fact, very few instances of consecutives in the chorales to which an orthodox theoretician would object. Some of Bach's methods of avoiding consecutives, on the other hand, would not always be accepted so readily. Probably the most common of these is the simple expedient of inserting a harmony note into one of the offending parts; the fifths in example 8(b), for instance, are often removed by writing a quaver D between the F sharp and the E in the bass line. Crossing of parts, as has already been mentioned, will often remove unacceptable fifths and octaves— or at least make them acceptable (see example 9)!

Example 9

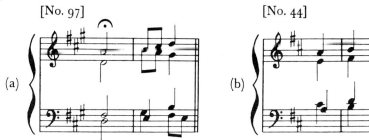

[No. 97] [No. 44]

(a) (b)

A rather less orthodox method of removing, or avoiding, consecutives is by using a suspension. Bach clearly did not subscribe to the textbook rule that 'any progression which is incorrect without a suspension is incorrect with one'. Nor is there any reason for the student to do so, provided he is quite certain that his practice follows Bach's, which is exemplified in the extracts which follow (see example 10). The suspensions in the first three of these progressions are clearly used to avoid fifths, and the procedure is quite

Example 10

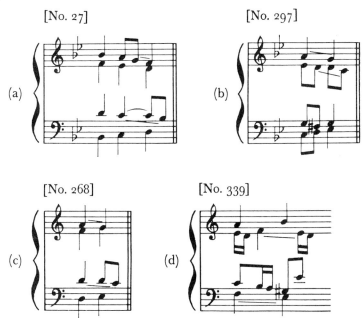

[No. 27] [No. 297]

(a) (b)

[No. 268] [No. 339]

(c) (d)

a common one in the chorales. Avoidance of consecutive octaves by the same method, however, is very rare, and the progression shown in example 10(d) is not one which should commend itself to the student.

TEXTURE

Leaving aside those chorales which receive some special treatment (often because they were originally part of a long cantata chorus), it is possible to distinguish three main kinds of texture in Bach's chorale harmonizations. One extreme is a plain setting with few or no unessential notes, examples of which have already been mentioned. The other is a complex proliferation of semiquaver movement, very often in conjunction with a melody somewhat longer than usual (see chorales nos. 132, 197, and 241). The third type, and by far the commonest, is the one towards which the student should first direct his attention. Here the lower parts move mainly in crotchets and quavers, with perhaps occasional semiquavers. Some quaver movement is essential for the typical Bach style, not only to provide interest in the individual voice parts, but also (and perhaps this is just as important) to lend fullness to the sonority.

No matter how many suspensions and passing notes are used, however, the basic texture remains harmonic. Some chorales, it is true, show an interest in contrapuntal possibilities (see chorales nos. 90 and 209), but these are rare and the student should not waste his time trying to introduce imitative phrases into the part-writing. Once the basic harmony has been worked out, beginning with the cadences, his main concern should be for sonority. This involves the use of unessential notes, as we have just stated, and also demands a careful regard for the spacing of the four vocal lines.

The most common error in this respect is to write a tenor part which is too low. Most students, unless corrected, will write for the tenor as though for a first bass voice, in spite of the fact that most tenor voices are comparatively limited in strength and quality below about middle C. Writing in short score, with the bass and tenor sharing the same stave and clef, no doubt aggravates the tendency, and the use of open score has much to commend it. (We know that Bach himself preferred his pupils to use open score for chorales.) A glance at the ledger lines in the printed copy, however, will usually be enough to persuade the student that low tenor lines are uncharacteristic. If not, then let him listen to the tenors soaring upwards in such places as the last line of 'O Lord, who dares to smite Thee?' in the *St Matthew Passion* (chorale no. 50 in the '371')

If Bach appears to lavish particular attention on his tenor lines, there is a good reason for it. The chorale melody itself, because it was designed for congregational use, is necessarily low-pitched as a rule. Consequently the altos must also use the lower part of their range, for to allow the two parts to cross would be to spoil the contours of the chorale melody. Thus the tenor is the only voice which can stand out from the texture without detriment to the given soprano, and the shaping of the tenor part is something which should always exercise the care and imagination of the

student. Although it should not extend above , the tenor should

reach that note and those just below it fairly often. The wide gap between tenor and bass which frequently results does not detract from the sonority, although wide gaps between other parts tend to do so. They may, however, be desirable from time to time in the interests of good part-writing. Crossing of alto and tenor lines is in the Bach style, provided it is done neatly and with audible reason. Tenor and bass lines also cross, but it is important to bear in mind that in such cases Bach always envisioned the doubling of the bass one octave below, either on 16-feet organ stops or in the orchestral basses. Thus the bass part, even when written above the tenor, always remains the true bass of the harmony. On the whole, the student would be well advised to avoid crossing the two lowest parts, at least until he is well familiar with Bach's methods here. Even in Bach's workings it is not very often found.

MODAL CHORALES

It is not often that the student is asked to harmonize a modal chorale, but there are quite a lot of them in the '371' and it is very desirable that he should know something of Bach's methods of dealing with them. It will not be necessary to give a detailed account of the modal system, and those to whom it is unfamiliar need only know that the Dorian, Phrygian, Mixolydian, and Aeolian modes can be represented as extending from D to D, E to E, G to G, and A to A respectively (see example 11). Of these, the first two and the last one are quite commonly found, the most frequent being the Dorian and the least used the Mixolydian.

Example 11

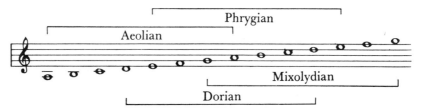

Many of the modal melodies found their way into the Lutheran Church from folksong or from Roman Catholic plainsong, but Bach makes no attempt to treat them in an archaic style. He does not try, in other words, to imitate the harmony of Palestrina or earlier composers. Rather the reverse in fact. Bach treats his modal chorales in such a way as to force them into a tonal system of harmony, at least as far as it is possible to do so. In the case of the Dorian and Aeolian modes this is not difficult, since they closely resemble our D minor and A minor scales, respectively. The problem of recalcitrant notes in the melody is usually solved by adroit modulation. A good example of Bach's methods is chorale no. 110. Here, a Dorian melody has been transposed down one tone, but the key-signature of only two flats cannot disguise the clear feeling of C minor which the harmony conveys.

Modal contours are not always smoothed away as easily as this. Chorale no. 162, for example, appears to begin in D minor and to end in E major (actually the dominant of A minor). The Phrygian mode gives rise to special problems, mainly because of the F natural with which the cadence is approached. In this case, Bach has to be content with an ending which, in terms of major and minor tonality, suggests the dominant chord. To avoid the abrupt and 'unfinished' effect which the Phrygian cadence has upon ears not tuned to modal harmony, he usually draws out the cadence with suspensions—a practice which, as we have observed earlier, he usually avoids elsewhere (see chorales nos. 10, 16, 56, 81, and 352).

The student faced with the task of harmonizing modal chorales will not go far wrong is he treats them tonally (as far as is possible) in accordance with the following observations of Bach's own practice:

Dorian chorales are treated as though in D minor (or its transposed equivalent);

Phrygian chorales are treated as though in A minor (or its transposed equivalent), ending with an imperfect cadence and usually with a suspension:

Mixolydian chorales are treated as though in either G major or C major (or their transposed equivalents). In the latter case, the ending will be 'imperfect' and suspensions will again be desirable;

Aeolian chorales are treated as though in A minor (or its transposed equivalent).

In conclusion, one can only emphasize again the importance of close personal study of the Bach models. Unlike the 48 Preludes and Fugues, the Two-part Inventions, and many of the chorale preludes, they were not written with any didactic intention, and yet they contain an immense amount of valuable instruction for the enquiring mind. If the present survey has in any way helped the reader towards a greater awareness of their value it will have served the sole purpose for which it was written.

EXERCISES

FORKEL tells us that when Bach himself set exercises in chorale harmony for his own students he 'at first set the basses himself and made the pupils invent only the alto and tenor to them. By degrees, he let them also make the basses'. (See H. T. David and A. Mendel, *The Bach Reader* (New York, 1945), p.329.) The practice is one which should commend itself to students today, and particularly to those who, in their 'pre-chorale' training, have perhaps been negligent in their attention towards the spacing and movement of middle parts. Before attempting exercises 1 to 3 the student is advised to read again the remarks on chorale texture on pages 24 to 25; his finished workings should be compared with Bach's own. For those who feel they need more practice than these exercises provide, the 69 chorale melodies with figured bass, included in many editions of Bach's Chorales (Terry's and Riemenschneider's among them), present admirable material.

Exercise 1

No. 9: *Ermuntre dich, mein schwacher Geist*

Exercise 2

No. 266: *Herr Jesu Christ, du höchstes Gut*

Exercise 3

No. 121: *Werde munter, mein Gemüte*

In exercises 4 to 14, the student is invited to add all three lower parts, using what he understands by 'normal' chorale harmony and texture. Comparison should again be made with Bach's own workings, and some at least of these exercises should be written in open score.

Exercise 4

No. 101: *Herr Christ, der ein'ge Gott's-Sohn*

Exercise 5

No. 129: *Keinen hat Gott verlassen*

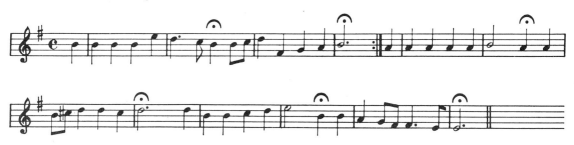

Exercise 6

No. 182: *Wär' Gott nicht mit uns diese Zeit*

Exercise 7

No. 24: *Valet will ich dir geben*

Exercise 8

No. 243: *Jesu, du mein liebstes Leben*

Exercise 9

No. 326: *Allein Gott in der Höh' sei Ehr'*

Exercise 10

No. 297: *Jesu, der du meine Seele*

31

Exercise 11

No. 322: *Wenn mein Stündlein vorhanden ist*

Exercise 12

No. 173: *O Herzensangst*

Exercise 13

No. 324: *Jesu, meine Freude*

Exercise 14

No. 260: *Es ist gewisslich an der Zeit*

Exercises 15 to 18 offer modal melodies. Before attempting to harmonize them, students should read again the remarks on Bach's handling of modal chorales (see pages 26 to 27).

Exercise 15

No. 187: *Komm, Gott Schöpfer, heiliger Geist*

Exercise 16

No. 166: *Es stehn vor Gottes Throne*

Exercise 17

No. 208: *Als vierzig Tag' nach Ostern*

Exercise 18

No. 110: *Vater unser im Himmelreich*

For the three chorales which follow the student is invited to pro-vide a more than usually chromatic harmonization. Since they are among the most widely admired of all Bach's chorale harmoni-zations, he would be well advised to commit the originals to memory. The chorale from which exercise 19 is taken brings to a close the first part of the *St John Passion*, and 21 is the most poignant of many settings of the same tune in the *St Matthew Passion*. Exercise 20 (from the Cantata no. 60, *O Ewigkeit, du Donnerwort*) is remarkable for the 'modern' sound of its harmonies, and was introduced, with Bach's own harmonization, by Alban Berg into the second movement of his Violin Concerto (1935).

Exercise 19

No. 83: *Jesu Leiden, Pein und Tod* (cf. also no. 106)

Exercise 20

No. 216: *Es ist genug; so nimm, Herr*

Exercise 21

No. 89: *O Haupt voll Blut und Wunden*

Finally, four examples in which the treatment goes beyond the normal requirements of chorale style so far as texture is concerned. In these, the style of the opening should be maintained throughout.

Exercise 22

No. 164: *Herr Gott, dich loben alle wir*

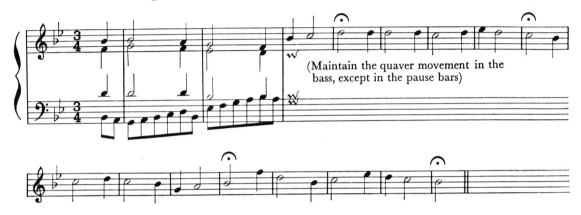

(Maintain the quaver movement in the bass, except in the pause bars)

Exercise 23

No. 331: *Wo soll ich fliehen hin*

[violin]

(Complete the harmonization for S.A.T.B., and the solo violin counterpoint, mostly in quavers)

Exercise 24

No. 339: *Wer nur den lieben Gott Läst walten*

(Include a fair amount of semiquaver movement)

Exercise 25

No. 152: *Meinen Jesum lass' ich nicht, weil*

(Maintain the bass quavers, except at cadences)

APPENDIX—INDEX OF CHORALES

The numbering of the chorales mentioned in the text and in the examples of this booklet has followed that in the editions of the *371 Chorales* published by Breitkopf & Härtel and by Schirmer. Those readers with other editions can quickly locate the relevant chorales with the aid of the following index, which relates the numbering in the '371' to that in other publications. Unfortunately, it has not been possible to mention every single volume containing Bach's harmonizations, although it is thought that most of the important ones at present available have been included; those working from editions not here listed will probably have little difficulty in identifying a chorale by means of its title alone.

Figures refer to the numbers of the chorales, except in the case of *Atkins*, where they indicate page numbers, and in the case of *B.-G.*, where they indicate the numbers of volume and pages. Abbreviations are used to distinguish the various editions as follows:

Breitkopf	*371 Vierstimmige Choralgesänge für Klavier oder Orgel oder Harmonium*, by J. S. Bach (Breitkopf & Härtel).
Riemenschneider	*371 Harmonized Chorales and 69 Chorale Melodies with figured bass*, by J. S. Bach, ed. Albert Riemenschneider (Schirmer, 1941).
Terry	*The Four-part Chorales of J. S. Bach*, ed. Charles Sanford Terry (Oxford University Press, 1929; new edition ed. Walter Emery, 1965).
Richter	*389 Choralgesänge für gemischten Chor*, by J. S. Bach, ed. Bernhard Friedrich Richter (Breitkopf & Härtel).
Smend	*Mehrstimmige Choräle*, by J. S. Bach, ed. Ludwig Erk; new and revised edition by Friedrich Smend (Edition Peters, 1932, 2 vols.).
Buszin	*101 Chorales harmonized by J. S. Bach*, ed. Walter E. Buszin (Schmitt, Hall & McCreary, 1952).
Ashby	*The Pianist's Book of Bach Chorales*, 100 Chorales chosen from Terry's complete edition by A. B. Ashby (Oxford University Press).
Atkins	*The Organ Works of J. S. Bach, book XX: The Chorales*, ed. Ivor Atkins (Novello).
Gessner	*60 Selected Four-part Chorales*, by J. S. Bach, ed. A. Gessner (Breitkopf & Härtel, reprinted from *Breitkopf*).
B.-G.	*Bachgesellschaft edition*, except vol. XXXIX (Breitkopf & Härtel).
B.-G. 39	*Choräle für vier Singstimmen aus der Sammlung von C.P.E. Bach:* Bachgesellschaft edition vol. XXXIX, ed. Franz Wüllner (Breitkopf & Härtel, 1892).
L.P.S.	Lea Pocket Scores No. 75. Miniature score edition of *B.-G. 39* (see above).

Breitkopf and Riemenschneider		*Terry*	*Richter*	*Smend*	*Buszin*	*Ashby*	*Atkins*	*Gessner*	*Bachgesellschaft*	*Bachgesellschaft Vol. XXXIX & L.P.S.*
1	Aus meines Herzens Grunde	31	30	30	30	—	—	—	—	17
3	Ach Gott, vom Himmel	8	5	7	—	—	—	3	32,43	—
8	Freuet euch, ihr Christen	110	105	86	75	28	—	—	7,394	—
9	Ermuntre dich	84	80	69	67	24	—	—	5(ii),59	—
10	Aus tiefer Not schrei' ich	32	31	31	9	9	8	—	7,300	—
11	Jesu, nun sei gepreiset	217	204	157	—	—	—	—	10, 58/35, 32[4]	—
15	Christ lag in Todesbanden	37	38	—	—	—	14	—	—	25
16	Es woll' uns Gott genädig sein	99	95	84	43	—	—	—	—	58
24	Valet will ich dir geben	324	314	—	—	82	74	24	—	162
27	Es spricht der Unweisen Mund	95	92	81	—	—	—	—	—	55
44	Mach's mit mir, Gott	241	237	—	—	—	—	—	—	124
50	In allen meinen Taten	300	292	230	—	—	—	50	4, 164	—
56	Christum wir sollen loben	47	42	44	84	12	16[2]	—	26, 20	—
60	Ich freue mich in dir	186	181	138	—	—	—	60	28,80	—
70	Gott sei gelobet	122	119	95	—	—	—	—	—	69
81	Christus, der uns selig macht	51	49	46	—	14	—	81	12(i),43	—
83	Jesu Leiden, Pein und Tod	206	192	145	—	—	—	—	12(i), 39	—
89	O Haupt voll Blut und Wunden	160[2]	164[2]	126[2]	—	—	—	89	4, 248[2]	—
90	Hast du denn, Jesu, dein Angesicht	125	231	179	34[3]	—	51	—	12(ii), 132	—
97	Nun bitten wir den heiligen Geist	262	256	198	—	—	—	—	33, 192	—
100	Durch Adams Fall	76[2]	73[2]	62[2]	100[2]	22[2]	23[2]	—	2, 252[2]	—
101	Herr Christ, der ein'ge Gott's-Sohn	132	127	101	—	34	—	—	33,88	—
102	Ermuntre dich	85	81	71	—	—	—	—	10, 126	—
103	Nun ruhen alle Wälder	307	295	232	—	—	—	—	2, 98	—
106	Jesu Leiden, Pein und Tod	207	193	146	—	—	—	—	12(i), 103	—
110	Vater unser im Himmelreich	326	320	249	46	—	75[4]	110	23,66	—
111	Herzliebster Jesu	170	169	130	56	—	—	111	12(i), 52	—
112	Wer nur den lieben Gott	381	373	283	—	—	—	112	20(i), 98	—
121	Werde munter, mein Gemüte	384	361	287	—	—	—	—	4, 173	—
122	Ist Gott mein Schild	197	216	166	—	46	—	—	20(i), 118	—
129	Keinen hat Gott verlassen	223	217	167	—	—	—	—	—	116
132	Kyrie, Gott Vater	231	225	—	—	—	52-54[5]	132	—	118
134	Du, o schönes Weltgebäude	75	71	60	—	—	—	134	—	48
139	Warum sollt ich mich denn grämen	348	335	260	—	—	—	139	5(ii), 124	—
140	In allen meinen Taten	192	211	162	58	—	—	—	—	114
149	Nicht so traurig, nicht so sehr	261	253	196	—	60	—	—	—	131
150	Welt ade! ich bin dein müde	365	350	274	—	—	—	—	5(i), 244	—
162	Das alte Jahr vergangen ist	58	55	51	—	18	19	162	—	35
164	Herr Gott, dich loben alle wir	133	129	—	87	35	—	164	—	73
166	Es stehn vor Gottes Throne	96	93	82	—	—	—	166	—	56
173	O Herzensangst, o Bangigkeit	294	284	—	—	69	—	—	—	147
176	Erstanden ist der heil'ge Christ	88	85	—	—	—	—	—	—	53
179[6]	Wachet auf, ruft uns die Stimme	342	329	256	17	86	82[7]	—	28, 284	—
181	Gott hat das Evangelium	120	116	—	—	—	—	—	—	66
182	Wär Gott nicht mit uns	343	330	257	—	—	—	—	2, 132	—
183	Nun freut euch, lieben Christen	268	261	202	69	63	—	—	—	135
184	Christ lag in Todesbanden	39[4]	41[4]	39[4]	15[4]	—	—	—	1, 124[4]	—
187	Komm, Gott Schöpfer	224	218	168	72	—	49	—	—	117
197	Christ ist erstanden	35/36	36/37	34/35	27	—	13	197	16, 214	24
205	Herr Gott, dich loben wir	137	133	—	—	—	—	205	—	75
208	Als vierzig Tag nach Ostern	23	22	—	—	—	—	—	—	14

Breitkopf and Riemenschneider		Terry	Richter	Smend	Buszin	Ashby	Atkins	Gessner	Bachgesellschaft	Bachgesellschaft Vol. XXXIX & L.P.S.
209	Dir, dir, Jehovah	70	67	—	—	21	—	—	—	46
214	Mitten wir im Leben sind	260	252	—	—	—	—	214	—	130
215	Verleih uns Frieden gnädiglich	333⁴	321⁴	253⁴	95⁴	—	—	—	26, 131⁴	—
216	Es ist genug, so nimm, Herr	94	91	80	82	26	—	—	12(ii), 190	—
219	O wie selig seid ihr doch	311	300	233	—	—	—	—	—	153
238	Es wird schier der letzte Tag	97	94	83	—	—	—	238	—	57
241	Was willst du dich	364	349	—	—	92	—	241	—	172
243	Jesu, du mein liebstes Leben	203	190	—	—	48	—	—	—	103
244	Jesu, Jesu, du bist mein	204	191	—	—	49	—	—	—	104
260	Es ist gewisslich an der Zeit	270	262	203	—	64	61¹	—	—	54
266	Herr Jesu Christ, du höchstes Gut	145	144	111	—	—	—	—	10, 298	—
268	Nun lob mein Seel den Herren	277	269	—	—	66	—	—	—	136
269	Jesu, der du meine Seele	198	186	142	—	47	—	—	—	100
270	Befiehl du deine Wege	158	161	121	—	—	—	270	33, 27	—
273	Ein feste Burg ist unser Gott	79	76	65	—	23	—	—	18, 378	—
278	Wie schön leuchtet der Morgenstern	392	375	—	—	99	—	—	—	183
283	Jesu, meine Freude	213	199	150	—	—	—	—	39, 75	—
294	Herr Jesu Christ, du höchstes Gut	146	142	110	—	—	—	—	24, 80	—
296	Nun lob mein Seel den Herren	278	270	—	—	—	—	—	—	137
297	Jesu der du meine Seele	199	188	143	—	—	—	—	18, 286	—
321	Wir Christenleut	396	379	301	—	—	86	—	7, 377	—
322	Wenn mein Stündlein vorhanden ist	368	353	—	—	—	—	—	—	175
323	Wie schön leuchtet der Morgenstern	394	376	298	—	—	85⁴	—	35, 69	—
324	Jesu, meine Freude	212	197	152	—	—	—	—	20(i), 24	—
326	Allein Gott in der Höh sei Ehr	17	13	17	—	5	4	—	23, 116	—
327	Jesu, nun sei gepreiset	218	205	156	—	—	—	—	37, 257	—
331	Wo soll ich fliehen hin	30	27	26	—	—	—	—	28, 164	—
334	Für deinen Thron tret ich hiermit	136	132	103	—	—	—	—	—	74
339	Wer nur den lieben Gott	378	371	280	—	—	84	—	35, 292	—
345	O Haupt voll Blut und Wunden	162	165	127	—	—	—	345	5(ii), 36	—
352	Es woll' uns Gott genädig sein	98	96	—	—	—	—	352	—	59
356	Jesu, meine Freude	208	195	—	—	—	—	—	—	105
360	Wir Christenleut	395	381	302	—	100	—	—	5(ii), 126	—
368	Hilf, Herr Jesu, lass gelingen	178	—	311	41	41	—	—	5(ii), 166	—

¹Minor third lower.   ²Tone lower.   ³Semitone lower.   ⁴Tone higher.
⁵Minor third higher.   ⁶Note values halved in *Breitkopf*.   ⁷Note values halved.